THE LITTLE BOOK OF AGILE WISDOM

Agile culture, mastered and manifested

Jérôme Grimm, Anton Podokschik

B/S

BIS Publishers

Borneostraat 80-A

1094 CP Amsterdam

The Netherlands

T +31 (0)20 515 02 30

bis@bispublishers.com

www.bispublishers.com

ISBN 978 90 636 9698 6

For all our loved ones.

CONTENTS

INTRODUCTION

Our journey

Over the last ten years, we have navigated through the dynamic world of Agile. We have coached and led numerous Agile teams, guided large organisations on their Agile journey and empowered many leaders to embrace an Agile leadership approach. Throughout these years, we have witnessed both, successes, and setbacks. A critical factor distinguishing successful Agile teams from the rest is the genuine adoption of an Agile culture. While many teams excel in Agile processes, frameworks, and methodologies, true success lies in also embodying and live an Agile culture. We have seen that teams that fully adopt this culture are the ones that thrive in their endeavours, realising the full potential of Agile principles.

This book is born from those experiences and aimed at leaders like you.

Whether you are a Scrum master, a release train engineer, an Agile organisational unit lead, an Agile coach, or have any other Agile leadership role, it should help you to guide your team to a truly Agile culture.

Adopting an Agile culture is more than just a strategic shift. It is a paradigm change that can be both challenging and rewarding. As leaders, you play a crucial role in leading this change. It is imperative, therefore, to understand the key driving forces behind an Agile culture. Let us explore its essence and look into the core elements that define and shape it.

The essence of Agile culture

Defining an Agile culture can be challenging, with many interpretations of its nature. This book chooses an approach centred on the following six key areas where leaders should actively engage with their teams.

1 **FOCUS ON VALUES** – Build your team culture based on Agile values. Encourage your team to align every action with these values.

2 **FOCUS ON LEADERSHIP** – Ensure your team experiences supportive leadership. Be an Agile role model.

3 **FOCUS ON EFFECTIVENESS** – Help your team focus on the customer. Encourage them to prioritise tasks that directly create value.

4 **FOCUS ON INNOVATION** – Support your team to seek out and try new ideas. Make innovation an ongoing objective.

5 **FOCUS ON PRODUCTIVITY** – Drive with your team efforts to optimise throughput. Streamline workflows and reduce waste.

6 **FOCUS ON IMPROVEMENT** – Empower your team to constantly evolve. Establish a continuous learning environment.

We have witnessed firsthand how teams that integrate these pillars survive and thrive, unlocking Agile's full potential. These focus pillars collaboratively contribute to the vibrant manifestation of an Agile culture. Now, the question arises: How do you make these pillars stand within your team?

Culture evolution through behaviour change

Cultural change is a subtle art. While culture cannot be directly reshaped, altering behaviours can influence and gradually transform it. If you want to effectively initiate these behavioural changes, it is crucial that you cultivate an environment where the new behaviours are encouraged and actively rewarded. Moreover, it is important that you recognise that teams require time to adapt to these new behaviours. Overburdening them with too much change at once can be counterproductive. Therefore, pacing the introduction of new behaviours is essential for you and your team to ensure the change is sustainable and deeply integrated within your team's culture.

The crucial role of leadership in cultural transformation

Leadership plays a pivotal role in shaping a team culture. As a leader, you are both the guardian and a primary influencer of the team culture. You are responsible for setting boundaries, exemplifying behaviours, and steering the team towards desired practices and norms. Your actions and decisions have the power to either reinforce the current culture or challenge your team to evolve. This involves not just directing but also listening, adapting, and growing alongside your team. Effective leaders understand that their behaviour sets the tone for the team's behaviour. Therefore, your commitment to truly embodying the principles of an Agile culture is essential in guiding your team through their transformative journey.

How we support you on the cultural journey

This book is designed to help you on that cultural journey. It offers guidance on how to foster an Agile culture by tangibly working with your team on behaviours along the six mentioned focus areas. Each area has a collection of eleven key behaviours essential for your team's cultural evolution.

Recognising the power of quotations to inspire and stick in mind, we have paired each behaviour with a resonant quote. Many of these quotes, often from influential leaders in Agile transformations, have helped organisations and teams on their transformation journey. Some have become a mantra, and we have heard them in the hallways during an Agile transformation within the organisations we have worked with. For instance 'Obstacles are not in the way, obstacles are the way' has been a recurring refrain, encouraging teams to adopt a growth mindset when faced with challenges.

For every quote, we provide a context, explain its relevance in an Agile environment and augment it with a hands-on exercise for practical application. Furthermore, the pictures accompanying each quote aim to trigger an additional reflection process on a visual level. This approach ensures that the wisdom imparted is inspirational and actionable, empowering you to lead your team to Agile excellence.

How to use this book

This book is designed in a modular fashion, offering flexibility in how you engage with its content. Remember, cultural change is a journey, not a sprint. It is best to approach this book in bite-sized segments, integrating its lessons over time. Here are some tailored ways based on your role:

1. **For Scrum masters of new Agile teams:** Periodically select a quote and collaborate with your team to dive into its meaning. Use the accompanying exercise to bring the concept to life. Progress through the chapters systematically to build a strong foundation.

2. **For Agile coaches addressing specific cultural topics:** Identify a quote that aligns with the cultural topic you want to address. Ensure that the area you coach understands the quote's essence and implement the exercise to engage with the topic practically.

3. **For Agile leaders crafting learning journeys:** Use the chapters as a curriculum for your leadership team. Have leaders conduct exercises with their teams, then let them share outcomes and insights in leadership meetings to learn from each other.

4. **For Agile team members seeking personal growth:** Browse the book and find a quote that resonates with you. Reflect on how you can apply its insights personally and consider sharing your thoughts with a colleague over a coffee break.

5. **For Scrum masters enhancing team retrospectives:** Review the exercises to find one that could open new perspectives for your team. Introduce the exercise in your next retrospective to facilitate meaningful discussions. Choose every retrospective a different exercise.

6. **For Agile transformation leads strengthening their narrative:** Select quotes that bolster your transformation story. Use these quotes recurringly in your communications for impactful storytelling.

Each chapter, quote and exercise in this book is an opportunity to inspire, challenge, and grow. Leading a team, coaching others, driving a transformation or being on your own Agile journey, let these pages be your guide to cultivating a vibrant Agile culture.

FOCUS ON VALUES

Agile teams emerge as a key element to success in today's rapidly evolving business landscape. They are characterised by for constant innovation, adaptability, and swift response to change. These teams are encouraged and required to self-organise, adapt fast, and demonstrate resilience and flexibility. To do so, a robust team culture is crucial.

Especially self-organisation is just possible if a team has common ground through a team culture lived by all team members. Such a culture is rooted in a set of Agile core values, like commitment to collaboration, ownership, adaptability, and continuous improvement. Furthermore, such a culture thrives on feedback and iterative progress, focusing on rapidly delivering outcomes to the customer. Values (e.g. transparency, open communication etc.) are essential, as they foster trust and unity among team members.

Ultimately, a strong foundation of Agile values equips a team to respond to changes with remarkable agility while fostering a shared sense of ownership and responsibility toward a common goal. This is why building a robust Agile team culture based on values is not a choice, it is the very foundation upon which the success of Agile and self-organisation rests.

BE IT,
INSTEAD OF
DOING IT

Agile is more than just following a process.

Context

Agility is not just about following a process or a framework. Cultivating the right mindset is crucial to maximise the benefits of Agile. While processes provide structure to us and our teams, the mindset ensures that frameworks and methods come to life and unleash their potential.

An Agile mindset transforms how we approach challenges, emphasising adaptability, continuous learning, and collaboration. It drives us to solve problems proactively, remain flexible amidst change, and focus on people. Relying solely on processes feels mechanical, but with a genuine Agile mindset, we can follow procedures and passionately embrace their core principles, fostering true innovation and efficiency in what we do.

Team Exercise

Engage in a team discussion centred around core Agile values (e.g. collaboration, customer-centricity, continuous learning, empowerment, or transparency). Let the team rate its current alignment with these values and define a target score. Define and plan actionable steps to enhance alignment in areas needing improvement. Repeat the discussion regularly.

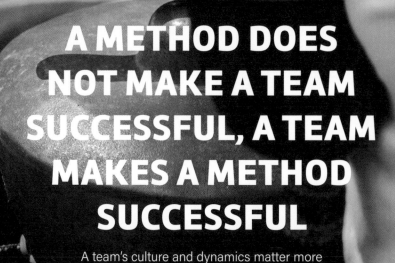

A METHOD DOES NOT MAKE A TEAM SUCCESSFUL, A TEAM MAKES A METHOD SUCCESSFUL

A team's culture and dynamics matter more than the specific method they choose.

Context

While Agile methodologies offer structured guidance, it is important to remember that the success of these methods depends on the team's execution and adaptation. As leaders, we need to understand that a method alone will not make our teams successful. It is the combination of the team's mindset and culture and its understanding of the method that genuinely determines its effectiveness.

For that, our teams should comprehend the underlying principles and the rationale behind the method. This understanding enables our teams not just to apply the method but to master it by continuously optimizing and adapting it to their unique environment and needs.

Team Exercise

Conduct a reflection meeting on your team's most recent successful application of Agile methods. Document the key behaviours and practices that contributed to this success. Repeat the exercise focusing on failure and compare it with success. Select the most applicable key behaviours and discuss strategies for applying them to future Agile methods.

WE ARE WHAT WE REPEATEDLY DO

Our stakeholders gain confidence in us
if we deliver outcomes regularly.

Context

In Agile teams, reliability and predictability are forged through a relentless commitment to delivering outcomes continuously and consistently. This consistency is crucial, as it builds trust within the organisation, assuring our teams can meet their commitments. Such confidence is foundational for our stakeholders to plan future work and trust in a timely delivery.

To maximise this trust-building process, our teams should establish a regular cadence, adhering rigorously to iterative delivery cycles and trying to keep these cycles as short as possible. This approach leads to more frequent opportunities for learning and improvement, thereby increasing the teams' overall predictability and reliability.

Team Exercise

Facilitate a team meeting to discuss adherence to commitments over the past two months, ideally using your collected predictability metrics. Derive and document success criteria. Based on documented success criteria, collaboratively brainstorm, document, prioritise and implement strategies for enhancing reliability and improving the team's ability to fulfil promises. Remind the team regularly to use the documented strategies.

KNOW THYSELF

Self-awareness is key for high performing Agile teams.

Context

Self-awareness is a cornerstone in building a thriving Agile team environment. It equips our team members to accurately identify their strengths and areas for growth. Fostering a safe and trusting atmosphere where such personal insights can be openly discussed helps to leverage each member's unique abilities effectively, enhancing team synergy.

Collective self-awareness within our teams is equally important. It allows teams to comprehensively understand their combined strengths and weaknesses. With this collective insight, the team can strategically focus on areas that require growth and development, enhancing its overall effectiveness. By embracing both individual and collective self-awareness, our teams position themselves for continuous success.

Team Exercise

Create a skill matrix with your team. List all the skills (e.g. front end, testing, etc.) you need to deliver your product and discuss what skill levels you need to be successful. Let all the team members rate themselves on these skills (scale from 1 (beginner) to 5 (expert)). Compare the required skill levels with the team skill levels and define and plan actions to close the gaps or to grow as a team. Repeat regularly.

ALONE WE GO FASTER, TOGETHER WE GO FURTHER

Work and deliver as a team.

Context

Collaboration in an Agile team is crucial for several reasons. We combine our diverse perspectives, guaranteeing a comprehensive view of tackling challenges. Through our collective insights, we frequently discover more creative and impactful solutions.

Additionally, working together allows us and our teams to spot and address concerns promptly, leading to faster feedback. Collaboratively achieved objectives result in shared success. This fosters trust and transparency among us and our team members, ensuring we feel appreciated. This helps us becoming more adaptable and effective, resulting in a durable, and stable Agile team.

Team Exercise

Analyse your team's work of the last two months. Discuss the reasons behind the non-achieved objectives with regards to team collaboration and discuss what each team member could have done better. Derive general rules and behaviours, which are applied by all team members. Agree on these rules and behaviours and inspect and adapt them regularly in future.

SHARING IS CARING

Continuous sharing creates a culture of trust
and psychological safety.

Context

In Agile, we recognise that collaboration extends beyond mere task execution and schedule adherence. It is about creating a culture where teams openly share ideas, feedback, successes, and even failures. When team members engage in open and transparent sharing, it facilitates learning from each other, leverages the group's collective wisdom, and fosters an environment of trust, psychological safety and appreciation. This culture of openness and sharing promotes not just the exchange of knowledge but also encourages empathy and understanding among team members, leading to a strong team bond.

Team Exercise

Schedule a weekly or fortnightly meeting dedicated to sharing. Grant preparation time and assign each team member five to ten minutes of meeting time to share something they have learned in the past two weeks with the entire team. After sharing, discuss how all team members can apply these learnings and plan improvement if necessary.

TRUST IS THE KEY
THAT UNLOCKS
POTENTIAL

Self-organisation requires trust to be successful.

Context

Trust is a cornerstone in empowering our team members to collaborate, innovate, and take ownership of their work. It fosters autonomy, enabling team members to have confidence in each other's capacity and skills to make sound decisions without constant oversight.

Trust creates a safe environment for our team members to take calculated risks and introduce fresh ideas, free from the fear of criticism or judgment. Additionally, it facilitates open and constructive feedback exchange, aiming for mutual growth and enhancing overall team performance. These dynamics contribute to the formation of high-performing Agile teams.

Team Exercise

Engage your team in a trust equation consideration exercise. Let the team explore its dimensions of credibility, reliability, intimacy, and self-orientation. Encourage ideation on how these dimensions can be positively influenced within your team's context. Let the team collectively select the most impactful levers and derive actionable team strategies to strengthen trust.

THE WORLD ONLY GETS BETTER IF PEOPLE SPEAK UP

Psychological safety is the foundation for team members to share their thoughts.

Context

Creating an environment where team members feel secure in sharing concerns and being genuine is critical for team success. Engagement and collaboration thrive when team members feel their opinions and contributions are appreciated and valued. Such a supportive atmosphere enhances the team's resilience and overall performance, enabled through the exchange of crucial feedback, constructive dialogues and the possibility to challenge the status quo.

As leaders, nurturing psychological safety means ensuring our teams feel safe to experiment, express ideas, and participate in an open dialogue. This approach is fundamental to achieving Agile success, as it encourages a culture where every voice can lead to progress, innovation and improvement.

Team Exercise

Perform a workshop on the five critical aspects of psychological safety, vulnerability, collaboration, courage, inclusion, and trust. Let team members rate the team on a scale from 1 to 10 in each aspect. Harmonize results, decide what aspects the team wants to improve and define three action items to implement. Perform the workshop regularly to establish a transparent communication behaviour.

SKILL IS SILVER
ATTITUDE IS GOLD

The right attitude transforms multiple team members
into a cohesive unit.

Context

For self-organized teams to be successful, having a healthy team culture is vital. While the skills and expertise of team members are undoubtedly crucial, it is their attitude that truly shapes the team's culture and effectiveness. A positive and constructive attitude is invaluable, characterized by effective collaboration, open communication, and a willingness to embrace failures as opportunities for growth. This mindset fosters an environment where team members not only apply their skills but also contribute to a supportive and adaptive team culture. It is the combination of skill and the right attitude that transforms a group of talented individuals into a high-performing unit.

Team Exercise

Create a list of specific Agile attitude aspects (e.g. collaborate effectively, learn continuously, experiment permanently, etc.) and have the team appraise each member. Discuss the results with each team member and let each team member select one aspect to improve. Conduct regular individual progress reviews while maintaining confidentiality.

DRINK YOU OWN CHAMPAGNE

Only expect from others, what you do yourself.

Context

A robust Agile team culture is anchored in leaders who lead by example. By embodying desired behaviours aligned to the Agile values, we set a powerful example, fostering a culture of integrity and reliability. This consistency in actions and words fortifies the team's belief in Agile and inspires members to imitate and embody the exemplified behaviours.

On the contrary, when leaders espouse Agile values but revert to traditional, hierarchical leadership practices, it leads to demotivation and even dysfunction within the team. Therefore, it is imperative for us to not only advocate Agile values but to actively live them.

Team Exercise

Inquire with your team members to anonymously assess your integrity on a scale from 1 to 10. Additionally, request team members to provide an example illustrating instances where you expect certain behaviours from the team, even when you may not exhibit those behaviours themselves. Derive action items and transparently share them with the team.

DON'T DO IT FOR THE SAKE OF DOING IT

Agile is not a destination, Agile is a journey.

Context

While Agile has proven to be very effective in many contexts, its implementation without clear objectives can lead to inefficiencies, lack of accountability, confusion, or frustration. Before embarking on an Agile journey, we and our teams must establish well-defined goals for the change. These objectives might range from enhancing efficiency and having more satisfied customers to increasing adaptability to market changes.

Regular reflection and alignment against these initial objectives is key to ensuring that the Agile practices are effectively leveraged to meet the desired outcomes. This focused approach prevents us and our teams from losing sight of their ultimate ambition and promotes a sustainable and purpose-driven adoption of Agile principles.

Team Exercise

Create an Agile vision board together as a team. Let pairs create Agile vision boards, creatively illustrating the significance of Agile and impact measurement for the team. After debriefing, vote as a team to select the best vision. Refine the chosen board as a team and have the entire team agree on and commit to it.

FOCUS ON LEADERSHIP

It is an often-heard misconception that self-organised Agile teams do not need leadership. They just need a different type than traditional teams. Agile leadership is not about command and control but understanding and facilitating what teams need to succeed. It is about having a systemic end-to-end view and about shaping an organisational system that supports and amplifies Agile practices. Furthermore, leadership in an Agile environment is a distributed concept, shared among various members within the team rather than centred on a single individual. This approach fosters a sense of collective responsibility and empowers team members to take initiative.

Agile Leadership is threefold - personal, team-oriented, and organisational. Personally, Agile leaders are on a continuous journey of self-awareness and improvement. In relation to the team, Agile leaders act as mentors and coaches, guiding team members in Agile practices and fostering an environment of collective growth. On an organisational level, they aim to create conditions and influence the surroundings that allow Agile teams to thrive, ensuring a collaborative, uplifting, and empowered workspace.

Through these multifaceted views, Agile leaders are instrumental in cultivating a fertile ground where an Agile culture can grow and where teams excel in their self-organised endeavours.

A TRUE LEADER IS AN ACCOUNTABLE LEADER

Ownership and responsibility is with the leader.

Context

Leadership accountability cultivates trust. As accountable leaders, even if we empower the team and promote self-organisation, we avoid blame for setbacks or when things go awry. Instead, we take ownership of situations, focus on solutions, and lead problem-resolution efforts. Accountability manifests through regular self-reflection, transparent communication, adherence to team agreements and clear goal setting.

Such leadership not only fosters a culture of responsibility and trust but also encourages team members to mirror these values. This dynamic creates a synergistic environment where team member feels supported and motivated to contribute, driving the team towards collective success.

Team Exercise

Conduct a coaching crowd meeting to discuss the following questions with your peers: Are we avoiding accountability through delegation? Do we own our and our team's mistakes and share what we learned after resolving them? Let each peer answer the questions, and others share feedback. Share what you will implement until the next coaching crowd meeting.

ASPIRE TO INSPIRE

Only when teams are truly inspired, they find expression
to dimensions they never imagined possible.

Context

In Agile teams, self-organization thrives when combined with inspirational leadership. As inspirational leaders, we possess the unique ability to spark intrinsic motivation and serve as role models in various dimensions. We inspire our teams to rally around a collective purpose, igniting their passion for the mission. Simultaneously, we inspire them through our personal qualities, cultivating trust, commitment, and a sense of unity.

Inspirational leadership sustains team momentum, celebrate incremental successes, and nurture a united, engaged, and innovative environment. By fostering inspiration, we empower our teams to excel.

Team Exercise

Define inspirational leadership behaviour with your team. Let the team members define weekly inspirational leadership missions for you, packaged into envelopes. Open an envelope every week, fulfil your weekly missions and let your team award points to you. Encourage your team lead colleagues to join your challenge and track points on a leadership scoring board.

KNOW YOUR PREFERENCES, ACT ALONG YOUR COMPETENCES

Balance competencies and personal preferences
for effective Agile leadership.

Context

Everyone possesses personal deep-rooted preferences (e.g. 'Big Five Personality Traits') and learned competencies on how to act in various situations. Understanding the competencies required in specific scenarios and not solely relying on personal preferences is paramount.

As an Agile leader, it is essential for us to align our actions with our competencies, finding the balance between leveraging our strengths and skills and being guided by our personal preferences. This self-awareness and adaptability enable more effective leadership and ensure that our interactions with the team are driven by competencies and the situation's specific needs, promoting collaboration and success.

Team Exercise

Assess yourself on the 'Big Five Personality Traits' (agreeableness, openness, extraversion, conscientiousness and neuroticism) to gain insight into your preferences. Identify situations where these preferences are advantageous and situations where they might lead to challenges. In scenarios where your preferences may hinder you, pinpoint competencies that can help. Develop strategies to align your actions with these competencies.

EMPOWERMENT IS A JOURNEY

Agile leaders support and guide their teams to empowerment.

Context

As Agile leaders, we cultivate the growth of self-organized and self-empowered teams. This transformation is not a swift change but a gradual and ongoing journey. Our role is to provide guidance through enablement and to create a nurturing and supportive environment that encourages team members to take ownership and responsibility.

Empowerment is a process of continuous learning and adaptation. It is about encouraging teams to make decisions, learn from outcomes, and progressively build confidence and competence. The road to empowerment is a series of small, deliberate steps, each contributing to the team's autonomy and effectiveness.

Team Exercise

Run an empowerment meeting with your team. For that, align on the following three dimensions: the desire to take responsibility, the possession of the necessary skills to exercise responsibility, and the permission to do so. Let the team examine its responsibilities and evaluate which of the three dimensions are fulfilled and where gaps exist. Define actions for you and the team and review the progress regularly.

DELEGATION IS A
TWO-WAY STREET

Mutual agreement forms the cornerstone of successful delegation.

Context

In an Agile environment, as leaders, we can only succeed if we delegate decision-making power and accountability to our teams. However, delegation is not one-sided but a collaborative effort between us and our teams. We can give decision power and accountabilities to the team members, but they also need to accept them.

Teams will commit to the delegated accountability only if they have a clear understanding, the relevant skills, and well-defined boundaries. Before keeping team members accountable, we first must discuss and agree on the respective topic of delegation. These aspects are making delegation a partnership where leaders and teams share the road to success.

Team Exercise

Review all delegated accountabilities with your team. For each delegation item, engage in a collective analysis with the team to assess if the goal was precisely defined, whether the team possessed the requisite skills and boundaries were clearly established. Derive improvement activities.

MAKE EMPOWER
YOUR SUPERPOWER

Ensure your team is equipped for success in all endeavours.

Context

When we trust our teams and equip them with the necessary skills, their engagement surges, and spaces for innovation open up. To empower effectively, we must not only instil trust but also provide the necessary resources, articulate the organisation's overarching objectives, and delegate authority and responsibility. This process is dynamic, enriched by the inclusion of regular feedback loops and acknowledgement of achievements. By embracing empowerment as a guiding principle, we become a catalyst for our team's evolution, fostering a culture of innovation and sustained success. This not only helps our teams but also strengthens the entire Agile ecosystem.

Team Exercise

Create a survey for your team on obstacles affecting its goals. Analyse responses and identify where and how you should provide resources or delegate authority responsibility to overcome obstacles. Share and discuss the findings with the team and trigger and monitor improvement steps.

WATER ALWAYS
FINDS A WAY

Define the outcome and trust the team to find its way.

Context

In the modern business landscape, organisations and their teams frequently operate in environments characterised by uncertainty. In these dynamic settings, as leaders, we need to recognise that we can neither predict the future nor micromanage every step to success. Instead, we should trust the team's ability to navigate challenges and discover the most effective route toward a defined goal. By providing a clear vision that serves as the team's 'north star' and clearly defined guardrails, we empower the team to adapt, pivot, and chart their way to a successful outcome, mirroring the resilience of water in its unwavering journey to find its course.

Team Exercise

Discuss currently existing guardrails with your team. Explore whether they are aligned with the vision and whether they are beneficial or obstructive (i.e. too narrow or too wide) for the team's success. Identify where and how guardrails should be expanded or narrowed. Perform a confidence vote on the improvements and take action.

AUTONOMY IS NOT FOR FREE

Autonomy and alignment move in harmony.

Context

Team autonomy is a key driver for innovation, responsiveness, and engagement. However, autonomy does not function in isolation, it thrives when paired with alignment. Alignment ensures that while our teams have the liberty to chart their course, they do so with a collective vision and purpose aligned with the organisation's overarching goals.

This balance between autonomy and alignment is underpinned by mutual trust. We believe in each other's ability to drive towards organisational goals autonomously, and our teams trust that we give clear direction. Together, autonomy and alignment form the backbone of effective Agile teams.

Team Exercise

Conduct an autonomy-alignment-compass exercise with your team. Let members reflect on the last month, focusing on how they feel on autonomy versus team alignment. Every team member should set a dot on a compass diagram. Reach team consensus on the desired balance point on the chart and brainstorm strategies that will bring the team closer to it.

WALK THE TALK

Teach others through your own actions.

Context

In an Agile environment, a 'doing' culture is desired. Instead of merely instructing team members, we as leaders should lead by example. By consistently demonstrating desired behaviours, we shape our teams' culture, providing a clear path for the team members to follow suit.

Simultaneously, we empower our team members by exemplifying hands-on activities (e.g. effective problem-solving, successful initiative planning, efficient execution, etc.). This proactive enablement approach fosters experiential learning, ensuring our team members gain relevant, real-world insights, which is a crucial asset in fast-paced Agile settings.

Team Exercise

Initiate a team discussion focused on the effectiveness of team members in demonstrating the 'walk the talk' model. Encourage the team to share experiences where they have exemplified desired behaviours including situations where others have copied these behaviours. This reflective dialogue promotes a collective understanding of how to lead by doing.

DON'T CHANGE PEOPLE, CHANGE THE SYSTEM

Agile leaders do not manage the people
but the system around the people.

Context

In an Agile environment, teams function as self-organised and empowered entities. As Agile leaders, our focus shifts from managing people and telling them what to do to managing the system surrounding the team, tailoring it for maximum effectiveness. We should establish this system with a focus on ensuring team members are motivated, feel empowered, have shared objectives, and are equipped with the proper skills and tools.

We also ensure that the team members feel safe and can flourish. With these aspects in mind, our teams have the foundation to grow and find their way of delivering efficiently and effectively.

Team Exercise

Reflect with your team on the challenges it currently faces. Analyse and identify the system-related challenges. Discuss how to tackle these by adjusting the system in which the team operates. Initiate small-scale experiments with these changes and observe how the system responds and adjust if necessary. Repeat the reflection regularly to nurture systemic understanding among all team members.

DIVERSITY MULTIPLIES YOUR POTENTIAL

Diverse teams have a broader solution space.

Context

Within complex and dynamic environments, where the path to a solution is often unknown, diversity plays an important role. A team that combines many perspectives, varied approaches, diverse knowledge, and distinct personalities can explore a broader range of ideas and solutions and uncover creative pathways to objectives.

As leaders, we are responsible for cultivating teams with the right mix of skills and backgrounds. Moreover, in diverse teams, we must foster an atmosphere of mutual respect and understanding. When diverse talents and viewpoints converge harmoniously, the team's collective potential is greatly amplified, leading to richer, more innovative outcomes.

Team Exercise

One aspect of diverse teams is that teams need different personality types. Conduct an exercise where team members identify themselves as dreamers, doers, or challengers based on their personality traits. Discuss how these roles help and challenge team dynamics. Finally, develop strategies to leverage each type's strengths and mitigate potential conflicts.

FOCUS ON EFFECTIVENESS

Nowadays, many teams focus solely on delivering more efficiently instead of becoming more effective. Effectiveness is about doing the right things. Those that yield meaningful results for the customer, leading to a better and more relevant product. This requires teams to shift their focus from merely completing tasks and working towards milestones to delivering tangible client value. This so-called customer focus is a key part of an Agile culture.

Central to this approach is a relentless dedication to understanding and responding to the unique needs and expectations of customers, positioning them at the core of all business activities. This customer-centric philosophy compels companies to develop products that fulfil customer requirements and exceed their expectations, thereby cultivating customer loyalty.

Achieving this needs a clear, overarching vision that guides the team, and which is serving as a north star towards which all efforts are directed. This vision should encapsulate the value being created and the intended customer. With this clarity, team members understand their contribution to the customer's narrative. Regular customer engagement and feedback loops are vital, enabling direct validation of the product's value.

Combined with frequent delivery iterations, this strategy is exceptionally powerful. In addition, consistently measuring the created value is crucial. It is ensuring that teams remain on course or that they are pivoting as needed to maintain alignment with customer needs and organisational goals.

KNOW YOUR COUNTERPART

Agile focuses on the customer's needs.

Context

We need to ensure that our teams know their customers well. It helps to prioritise work that delivers value and ensures a product's relevance. It enhances the teams' ability to interpret feedback accurately and respond appropriately, fostering a trust-based customer relationship. Our teams can achieve this by continuously engaging with their customers through workshops, launching experiments and observing customer behaviour.

This continuous engagement allows our teams to refine their products and adapt to changing customer needs. By thoroughly understanding our counterparts, we position our teams to create solutions that resonate deeply with customer requirements and driving customer satisfaction.

Team Exercise

Identify your customers with your team and create a persona canvas for each customer group. As part of the canvas, come up with three main value drivers (i.e. what delivered work do our customers perceive as valuable?) and assess how much focus you are currently putting on them. Derive and plan actions to improve and increase the focus. Repeat the activity regularly to foster customer focus behaviour.

PURPOSE INSPIRES ACTION

A common purpose helps a team to focus
and guides them in the decision making.

Context

To ensure our teams are focused on stakeholder satisfaction, we must embed customer centricity into the teams' purposes. Purpose acts as a powerful motivator for action. It provides a clear direction to follow, resulting in an increased engagement of our team members.

Agile teams can align their daily tasks with larger goals when they clearly understand the 'why' behind their work. It enhances their dedication and the relevance of their output. We must ensure our teams have a customer-focused and inspiring purpose, which they review and discuss repeatedly to nurture a purpose-driven culture.

Team Exercise

Let each team member write their version of the team's purpose, based on their understanding. Ask them to share it and explain how they included the customer. Write the individual versions on index cards and rotate among team members, having each team members improving the purpose on the index card until all members edited all index cards. Agree on final version and celebrate with a team picture where everyone signs off, symbolising commitment. Display your purpose statement prominently.

MORE IS NOT ALWAYS BETTER

Do not focus on quantity of your work,
but on value for the customer.

Context

We often think that the more we give, the happier we make our counterpart. These beliefs may not be valid with customer satisfaction. Customers are not necessarily more satisfied if we deliver more, especially if it differs from what they expect or does not delight them. Instead, we must ensure that our teams understand what solves their customers' challenges, addresses their needs, or delights them. Then, the teams must work on it without paying attention to the quantity of the output. By prioritising quality and relevance over quantity, teams elevate customer satisfaction and foster a lasting, trust-based relationship with them.

Team Exercise

Discuss your output over the last two months with your team and customers. Link the output to your customer's challenges and needs and ask if your current work has delighted them along a value scale. Analyse the correlation between output and value. Derive and implement improvements to shift the team's focus from output to value of the output.

TAKE MORE THAN YOU GIVE TO GIVE MORE THAN YOU TAKE

Reduce complexity wherever possible.

Context

To delight customers, lean and easy-to-use products are essential. Our teams should focus intently on core product functionalities and actively remove non-added value features. Moreover, it is not only about product simplicity, process simplicity within our teams is equally important.

To establish such a simplicity culture, regular inspection and proactive simplification are essential. Teams must rigorously assess every feature, process, and practice, ensuring they directly contribute to customer satisfaction and team efficiency. By continuously eliminating non-essential elements, we help to increase customer value as much as possible.

Team Exercise

Analyse your product and the processes together with the team. Document different aspects increasing or reducing the complexity of your processes and product. Add them to a complexity compass with four quadrants (product/increasing, product/reducing, processes/increasing, processes/reducing). Discuss the quadrant results and define rules for avoiding items in the increasing quadrants and strengthening the reducing quadrants.

DO NOT GET LOST IN TRANSLATION

Teams need to have a direct exchange with their customer.

Context

If teams want to maximise the customer value they create, a deep understanding of the customer itself is essential. We need to ensure that our teams are as close to the customer as possible, minimising the need for intermediaries. While proxies can help gather and consolidate customer feedback, nuances and critical insights can be lost.

We should help our teams to engage directly with customers for an unfiltered exchange of input and ideas. This direct dialogue enables our teams to capture customer needs and preferences accurately, fostering a more precise and effective product development process.

Team Exercise

Set up a regular team and stakeholder connection meeting. Prepare your team for the meeting by introducing and discussing the requirements for the upcoming two months. Note questions and discussion points. During the meeting, provide guidance and grant time for discussions between the team and stakeholders using the prepared questions and discussion points.

BEYOND LISTENING THERE IS HEARING

Our customers do not care if we listen, they want to be heard.

Context

Listening to customers and demonstrating that we have heard and understood them is critical to success. When customers see that their feedback has been acknowledged and acted upon, it builds trust, which is fundamental to establishing long-term relationships. Customers feel valued and secure and are more likely to stay with us.

We can demonstrate that we understood our customers by communicating what we have heard and making visible changes based on that feedback. This could involve follow-up interactions with individual customers, public announcements about changes or updates on product improvements. The key is to close feedback loops with clear communication and action.

Team Exercise

Conduct a customer voice integration workshop with your team and customer representatives. Collect customer feedback from the last two months. Make small groups of team members and let them analyse feedback, and derive solutions. Let groups demonstrate to customer representatives how they responded to their feedback and let the customers rate their solutions. Discuss and agree on actions.

EFFORT IS NOTHING
WITHOUT DELIGHT

Satisfy your customer not only rationally, but emotionally.

Context

If we want to build a strong relationship with our customers, they need to be thrilled by our work. To do so, our teams must deliver delighting features on top of the expected basic requirements. While meeting basic requirements is essential, the unexpected, delightful elements truly emotionally engage customers. These elements often come as a pleasant surprise, exceeding expectations and creating memorable experiences. When working on products, our teams must categorise the requirements accordingly and deliver a good mix of both types. This approach leads to lasting loyalty and a stronger customer relationship.

Team Exercise

Categorise your current customer requirements with your team. Prepare the two categories (essential, delightful) in the form of blank posters. Break into pairs and let pairs grab each requirement, discuss it, and place it onto the appropriate poster. Debrief on the outcome and agree on the requirements categorisation. Nurture the categorisation behaviour by establishing a recurring categorisation exercise.

UNDERSTAND
WITH YOUR EYES

True analysis requires observation.

Context

We can only gather genuine customer feedback by observational insights. To understand if our products truly satisfy our customers' needs, we need to analyse our customers' everyday usage of our product. We can do this via the combination of behavioural analysis (e.g. product interaction levels), direct feedback (e.g. satisfaction surveys) and engagement metrics (e.g. sales trends). Observing our customers' natural interactions with our products allows us to identify unarticulated needs and pain points, enabling us to innovate and enhance our offerings in a way that truly resonates with and delights our customers.

Team Exercise

Organise an 'observe your customers' day. Let the team talk to customers and observe them using their products. By the end of the exercise, have every team member share their observation and develop an idea of how to improve the product. Organise such a day quarterly.

LOOP TO PERFECTION

Regular customer feedback helps the team to deliver value.

Context

Agile teams conduct regular review meetings with customers to demonstrate the progress of the team's work. However, the review has another fundamental purpose. It fosters a feedback culture and enables the team to collect feedback often and directly from the customers. Each feedback loop helps teams to understand if their course aligns with customer needs or if adjustments are necessary.

With that approach, teams prevent delivering unnecessary or low prioritized work, but rather gradually move towards the best solution for the customers. We should ensure that our teams seize these reviews as opportunities to present their achievements and actively involve customers in the process.

Team Exercise

Conduct an improvement workshop with your team and stakeholders. Discuss how to decrease the size of your work packages to shorten your feedback loop and identify customer feedback channel improvements to increase customer feedback quantity and quality. Agree and plan improvement activities. Reflect and improve on work package size and feedback channels regularly.

TRUE SUCCESS IS MEASURED IN THE VALUE WE CREATE

Objective value measurements help to steer towards success.

Context

Delivering customer value is a key focus of Agile teams. Nevertheless, the assessment of value delivery often relies more on intuition than objective measurement. To transcend this, our teams must implement effective ways to measure the value they create.

It is essential to set clear objectives based on the value metrics teams aim to influence and rigorously measure whether the expected value is achieved. If the outcomes differ from expectations, teams should be ready to pivot or adapt their approach. This approach ensures that customer value is not just an abstract concept but a consistently delivered reality.

Team Exercise

Conduct a value metric (re-)definition workshop with your team. Align on what value means for the customer and the team. Define how it could be measured, identifying existing or easy-to-tap into data sources. Define a baseline and set improvement goals for the upcoming two months. Monitor and review progress regularly and celebrate success.

THE "WHY" DRIVES THE "HOW"

Tie your efforts to the big picture.

Context

Nowadays, many teams define what they want to deliver without understanding the purpose behind it. This lack of understanding can lead to misaligned priorities and to the development of features that may not meet customer needs. As leaders, we should support our teams in the mindset shift to start with defining the 'why' before the 'what' and 'how'. We must ensure that they understand the purpose and objectives behind each task and that every effort is tied to the bigger picture. With this approach, our teams not only become more effective but also more engaged. Understanding the purpose behind the work fosters motivation and a deeper sense of commitment.

Team Exercise

Review with your team members all the work packages they are working on to ensure the 'why' behind the work packages is clearly defined for each. If not, explicitly add this information to every work package. Perform this exercise regularly for all work packages your team works on to establish a common understanding among all team members and improve the purpose of the work packages.

FOCUS ON INNOVATION

In today's fast changing world, where client needs shift rapidly, innovation must be more than an organizational department. It must be a fundamental part of every team's culture, so that the products and services of a company continue to thrive and remain relevant.

Creating an environment conducive to innovation requires providing teams with the necessary space and time to explore new ideas. A safe space for innovation, where team members are not penalised for failures but encouraged to learn from them, is crucial. As the future is often unpredictable, comfort with uncertainty and a non-linear path to progress is essential. Teams must be agile enough to adapt to various possibilities. A clear understanding of the team's ambitions, coupled with consistent testing and validation of new ideas, concepts and products, is the foundation to staying aligned with customer needs.

Innovation should be approached in both, micro and macro scales. Team members should be empowered to bring innovative solutions to their daily tasks, while also being given opportunities to experiment with larger, more transformative ideas. Above all, it is vital to recognise that innovation is an ongoing journey. What is innovative today becomes outdated in the future.

CHANGE IS THE ONLY CONSTANT

Expect and embrace a continuously changing environment.

Context

The world is changing faster than ever. The ever-shifting landscape demands a continuous influx of new ideas and adaptations. Embracing this reality, we can navigate our teams to success in such a dynamic environment. This involves cultivating an innovation culture, making space for creativity, and providing psychological safety to try new things, fail early and learn from them. We must understand that today's cutting-edge systems will inevitably become tomorrow's outdated technologies. Therefore, staying ahead requires a proactive approach to change, constantly evolving and reinventing to meet the ever-changing needs of our customers.

Team Exercise

Reflect on your stakeholders' changing requirements and priorities from the last two months. Document and analyse the changes, mapping how a change has led to a creative solution or an innovative approach to demonstrate the positive effect of change to the team. Identify and document approaches and methods that have helped you with these changing requirements and re-use them in the future.

WHERE DREAMS LEAD,
REALITY FOLLOWS

Breaking through conventional thought patterns
is the foundation of innovation.

Context

Many teams are stuck in their day-to-day work, often thinking in the same patterns they have always known. However, innovation arises not solely from systematic planning and execution but also from the sparks of visionary ideas. Our teams must be able to think outside of the box and break through their conventional thought patterns.

We must cultivate an environment that encourages dreaming and visualising potential futures. When teams are empowered to think expansively and imagine boldly, they break through the barriers of traditional thought processes. This shift in mindset paves the way for groundbreaking ideas and solutions, transforming dreams into reality.

Team Exercise

Conduct a 'postcard from the future' exercise with your team. Divide into two groups, each tasked with creating a postcard written by a fictitious customer five years in the future, describing how they perceive your future product. After the groups present their postcards, each team member proposes one actionable idea inspired by the presentations. Prioritise these ideas and start working on them.

THE PATH
WILL SHOW UP,
WHEN YOU ARE
ON THE WAY

Embrace uncertainty and
be able to rapidly adapt to changes

Context

Innovation often starts as a journey into the unknown, where the solution, and even the path, is initially unclear. Our teams should accept this uncertainty, start exploring, and try to reach their goal incrementally.

We should encourage and motivate them to experiment in different directions, incorporating flexibility and optionality into their approach and dare to abandon strategies that do not contribute to success. This helps our teams recognise that the path to a solution often becomes apparent through exploration and experimentation. As they iterate and learn, the direction towards the right solution will emerge.

Team Exercise

Run a workshop with your team on how the team cuts through uncertainty and complexity. Collect and analyse current practices and underlying challenges by answering the question 'how do we build flexibility and optionality into our work?'. Brainstorm solutions and process improvements.

EARLY PAIN
IS LESS PAIN

Failing early gives you time to react.

Context

Early testing helps our teams understand whether they are on the right path. If not, adjustments can be made with minimal cost and effort. Delaying testing until later stages significantly amplifies risks. By then, substantial time and resources may have been invested in a potentially misguided direction. We should encourage our teams to test their solutions early in the process and to embrace a mindset where early setbacks are seen as stepping stones to success.

By embracing early feedback, iterating rapidly, and being willing to pivot quickly, teams can refine their solutions more effectively, aligning closely with customer needs and reducing the overall risk of failure.

Team Exercise

Create and perform a questionnaire with your team on implementing and testing new ideas (e.g. how fast did we gather customer feedback for your idea? what did early customer feedback lead to?). Prepare and analyse the results together, connecting them to 'failing early' behaviours. Identify reasons preventing the team from failing early. Based on the reasons, define solutions and implement them.

JUST DO IT

Early testing is better than overanalysing.

Context

In the traditional project management approach, teams invest most of their time in analysis before taking action. This approach often delays the onset of tangible work, as it tries to anticipate every possible issue beforehand. However, many insights and solutions emerge only through active experimentation and feedback gathering. Therefore, we should encourage our teams and stakeholders to test ideas and gather feedback early. This requires our teams to break down work into smaller, manageable packages which can be rapidly developed, resulting in minimal viable output. The output is tested with their stakeholders. This approach accelerates development and aligns solutions more closely with actual user needs.

Team Exercise

Analyse your team's work over the last two months. Let team members prepare by illustrating the lifecycle of their work packages (i.e. when and how long have they analysed and implemented their work?). Break into small groups and identify where earlier testing would have been possible. Agree on practices and behaviours to enable earlier testing for future work and commit as team to foster those.

UNCERTAINTY DOES NOT LEAD TO FEAR, FEAR LEADS TO UNCERTAINTY

If you are afraid of uncertainty, you will end up in uncertainty.
If you embrace it, you will advance through it.

Context

Agile methods, processes and tools are helping our teams to cut through complexity and deal with uncertainty. But fear of uncertainty often prevents them from applying these methods, processes and tools accordingly, leading to risks, impediments and failure.

To prevent fear of uncertainty, we must support our teams in overcoming their apprehensions and accepting it as an integral part of the innovation process. We can do that by not blaming them for failed experiments, supporting them in reflecting on uncertainties, and celebrating successful navigation of complexity. Establishing these behaviours makes uncertainty a strength instead of a weakness and allows our teams to push boundaries.

Team Exercise

Document a list of four top uncertainties (e.g. not knowing the true size of a task, not having all information upfront, etc.) and distribute it among team members. Establish a 15-minute reflection meeting with your team at the end of the work week. Discuss which main uncertainty prevented the team from applying Agile methods and identifying and implementing improvements continuously as part of your delivery process.

IN STILLNESS WE GROW

Innovation thrives,
if given time and space.

Context

Nowadays, we all understand that innovation is a differentiator for success. Looking at large enterprises, we realise that cost efficiency and delivery pressure often impede innovation culture. Our teams do not have the time for innovation if they are constantly pressured to deliver.

We must enable our teams to practice innovation by establishing and nurturing the right environment and granting the necessary time to practice innovation. This requires appropriate planning, where our teams have free time for innovation and continuous rigour from all organisation members. Only if we dedicate time, block out the noise of daily work and focus on innovation we will advance from it.

Team Exercise

Analyse your team's current innovation culture. Place work packages from the last two months onto a flip chart and categorise them into innovation or non-innovation. Understand and note the actual effort per work package and the conditions for innovation work packages. Derive improvements to ensure innovation conditions and agree on a standard amount of innovation time for each team member per month.

KNOW WHEN TO LET GO

Let go of the idea, if it is not used.

Context

To make products better, our teams should think about more than just what new features should be developed. They also must understand and accept which features can be removed. This is not easy to accept because human beings tend to protect their ideas and concepts, trying to make them successful. Breaking this cycle requires continuous evaluation, assessing whether new and current features contribute to customer delight.

Our teams must actively seek and consider feedback and be confident in dropping an idea with negative feedback. The freed-up focus and time lead to new and better ideas. Only such a reflective mindset leads to a thriving innovation culture and ensures that products remain dynamic and relevant.

Team Exercise

Discuss with your team how many ideas/features they have dismissed due to customer feedback in the last two months. Understand customers' reasons and team's behaviours, trying to identify general rules and conditions for 'letting go'. Agree together on your top five 'letting go' team rules and review and adjust them regularly.

TO GET TO THE MOON YOU NEED TO AIM FOR THE STARS

Setting high aspirations leads to significant outcome.

Context

If our teams are genuinely innovative, achieving breakthroughs in thinking and execution is part of their culture. We and our teams must set high aspirations to achieve such significant outcomes. Therefore, we must motivate our teams not just to set objectives within easy reach but rather ambitious, even seemingly unreachable, goals that challenge the status quo. This mindset pushes our teams to innovate and grow their product in ways which might have remained undiscovered with more conservative goal setting. Such a strategy goes beyond incremental improvements but can push a team to achieve something groundbreaking.

Team Exercise

Reflect with your team on objectives from the last two months and categorise them into aspiring and realistic. Emphasise the purpose of aspiring objectives. Agree on separation criteria between aspiring and realistic and on the number of aspiring objectives for a given timeframe (e.g., one quarter). Inspect and adapt separation criteria and the number of aspiring objectives regularly.

THINK BIG
ACT SMALL

Set aspiring objectives but build
a realistic path and walk it step by step.

Context

Innovation happens when our teams think big and try to strive for greatness. Often, in their day-to-day work, they neither see the big picture nor have the time to think innovatively. We must encourage them to set ambitious goals and challenging their objectives if they need to be more aspiring. Conversely, it is equally important for our teams to realise that these aspiring ideas must be translated into tangible, manageable packages which can be tested with the customer. This approach ensures that while the vision is expansive, the steps are practical. Balancing grand aspirations with pragmatic execution is the cornerstone of a thriving innovation culture.

Team Exercise

Analyse the current objectives and solution paths with your team. Challenge the objectives and improve if they are not aspiring enough. Afterwards, agree on a good mix of realistic and aspiring objectives. Inspect the solution paths and improve if the steps are too large or unclear. Re-plan after improving the solution paths. Establish this exercise recurringly.

DAILY INNOVATION
YEARLY REINVENTION

Make innovation part of your daily work.

Context

While driving for innovative breakthroughs, daily innovation routines can set ourselves apart from our competitors. We should encourage our team members to think innovatively in their day-to-day work, ensuring they have dedicated time to brainstorming and exploring new ideas. We should create an environment where experimenting with small-scale changes is a norm. This leads to a continuous flow of innovation. While these innovations are minor on their own, cumulatively, they lead to significant transformations over time. By focusing on incremental innovation and regular improvements, our teams can collectively drive the evolution and reinvention of their product over a longer time horizon.

Team Exercise

Introduce the daily innovation timebox in your team. Ask your team members to block a short timebox (e.g. 15 minutes) for innovation every day, ideally always at the same time (e.g. at the end of business). Prepare and provide a lean documentation template, enabling team members to document and follow up on their ideas. Remind your team members in team meetings and emphasize the importance of this behaviour.

FOCUS ON PRODUCTIVITY

Efficiency is a cornerstone of an Agile culture, especially critical as teams frequently deliver to customers. Optimising the flow of work is key to promptly completing tasks enhancing customer satisfaction through efficient and timely delivery of products or services.

Efficiency manifests in various forms. Firstly, teams should focus on task completion rather than juggling multiple in-progress activities. Completing tasks frees up mental space, allowing teams to focus on new challenges. To maintain this focus, an adaptive approach to planning, accommodating changing requirements and customer needs is critical. Teams should understand the optimal number of tasks in progress, completing work sustainably and plan accordingly. Empowering team members to make informed decisions supports this dynamic environment.

Additionally, teams should strive for clarity in defining what 'done' means, balancing quality with practicality. Recognising tasks to avoid is equally important, as is directing efforts towards impactful activities. Measuring the flow of work is another critical component. By tracking and measuring, teams can identify bottlenecks and areas for improvement. Small, iterative experiments can be applied to observe the impact on these metrics directly, allowing for continuous refinement of processes.

In essence, efficiency in Agile teams is about smart work management, clear completion standards, adaptive planning, empowered decision-making, and a commitment to process improvement, ensuring that every effort translates directly into value.

STOP TALKING, START DOING

Agile teams do not plan and analyse for a long time,
they start implementing and testing new things.

Context

In an Agile environment, we expect our teams to prioritise quickly implementing and testing new ideas rather than spending much time in extensive planning and analysis. Such a proactive approach allows our teams to iterate, learn, and adjust in real time. This is particularly effective in adapting to evolving requirements and unexpected challenges.

By minimising the initial planning phase and focusing on hands-on development, teams can respond more quickly to feedback and changing market needs. It fosters a dynamic work culture where progress is continuously made through tangible actions.

Team Exercise

Conduct an analysis workshop with your team, breaking into groups of two and analysing the developed features from the last two months, where analysis took longer than usual. Let groups identify and document reasons and reflect on how the analysis time could have been minimised. Conduct a debriefing and define actions to shorten analysis time.

GUESSING IS FASTER THAN KNOWING

Estimation is about collecting enough information
to make good decisions, not collecting complete information.

Context

In Agile settings, while estimates are crucial, we expect our teams to avoid overly detailed analysis when planning future work packages. Teams should collect an appropriate amount of information to make a reasonable estimation while finding the right balance between the depth of detail and the time invested in estimation. An effective approach is to harness the team's collective knowledge. Our teams should use each member's unique insights, knowledge, and experience, which, when pooled together, often lead to excellent and reliable estimates. This approach ensures that teams can confidently commit to deliverables without exhaustive analysis.

Team Exercise

Evaluate different estimation methods (e.g. MoSCoW, Planning Poker, etc.) with your team. Let each team member prepare and present one estimation method, giving an overview and pointing out the advantages and disadvantages. Decide upon the most appropriate for your team. Apply the method, inspect regularly, and adapt if necessary.

COMMIT TO FINISHING, NOT ONLY TO STARTING

Finish what you started promptly and unleash the power of value.

Context

True creation of value occurs when work packages are fully completed. Therefore, we ensure that our teams not only enthusiastically initiate tasks but also are committed to seeing them through to completion. This not only frees up mental space but also ensures timely delivery of value.

We help our teams to resist the temptation of constantly starting new tasks or activities without completing existing ones. This discipline in finishing what the team members have started enhances the team's efficiency and contributes to a stronger sense of achievement and progress.

Team Exercise

Reflect with your team on the behaviour of starting new tasks while having multiple in-progress activities. Identify and discuss triggers for pulling new tasks instead of taking care of the in-progress ones. Define behaviours to finish in-progress tasks timely and rules for new tasks (e.g. you can only start to work on a new task if you do not have more than two in-progress tasks). Remind your team members of the behaviours and rules when they pull new tasks to ensure understanding and adherence.

DONE IS BETTER THAN PERFECT

Get things done so you can test them with your customer and adapt based on the feedback.

Context

Contrary to traditional approaches that emphasise perfection, Agile prioritises completion. We encourage our teams to focus on finishing tasks to a level where they can be effectively tested and evaluated by the customer. Recognising that customer feedback will inevitably lead to further iterations, we do not expect initial perfection.

We help our teams to find the right balance between sound quality and time invested. Having the courage to show a customer or a stakeholder a not necessarily 'perfect' but viable outcome not only leads to better products over time but also increases the productivity of our teams.

Team Exercise

With your team and stakeholders, define and agree on minimum quality standards for work you want to test with the customer. Therefore, analyse the work of the last two months and identify timely delivered features with sound quality. Document these features' characteristics (e.g. testing acceptance and level of documentation) and let the team and stakeholders commit to it, fostering a symbolic handshake between all parties.

LONG-TERM SUSTAINABILITY TRUMPS SHORT-TERM INTENSITY

Work in a sustainable pace to optimise value output.

Context

To ensure that our teams consistently deliver value, they must maintain a sustainable pace of work. This means setting realistic commitments that can be met without resorting to constant overtime or operating under extreme pressure. By fostering a sustainable work culture, our teams maintain higher productivity and have the time and space to engage in creative thinking, allowing continuous innovation and improvement.

Sustainable practices ensure that our teams' well-being is prioritised, leading to a more stable, engaged, and innovative workforce. Embracing sustainability over short-term intensity helps build resilient and durable teams capable of adapting to changes and challenges while continuously delivering high-quality work.

Team Exercise

Analyse how much planned work your team has delivered over the last two months. Discuss the analysis with your team and identify moments where the team felt overworked. Reach a consensus on how much work you will plan in the future to meet commitment without overwork. Use this technique to reflect regularly and adjust if there is a difference between planned and delivered scope.

LESS IS MORE

Agile maximises the amount of work not done.

Context

To optimise the delivered value, our teams must not only understand what adds value to our products but also identify elements that do not. These non-essential aspects should be deprioritised, allowing the team to concentrate exclusively on valuable contributions. By reducing such clutter, our teams have more time and can focus on the essentials, making them impactful. Embracing this mindset of simplicity, which emphasises doing less but essential work, makes our teams more efficient and achieve a higher overall value output.

Team Exercise

Introduce the simplicity challenge in your team. Let each team member describe how they avoided unnecessary tasks and how much time they saved. Agree on a winner with the most saved time and award the person. Thank all team members for their simplicity behaviour. Make this challenge an inherent part of your delivery process and ensure that you also review the delivered value as a balancing metric.

LIMITATION
LEADS TO
LIBERATION

The only limits that should exist,
are for your work in progress.

Context

Each team member has a finite mental capacity. This rule also applies to the entire team. Overloading our teams with too many concurrent tasks can diminish efficiency. Thus, it is crucial that our teams consciously limit the number of tasks in progress at any given time.

This can be achieved through deliberate experimentation and adjustment, discovering the sweet spot where the workload is manageable, yet the throughput is high. Imposing thoughtful constraints on the number of active tasks not only streamlines workflow but also fosters a more liberated and focused work environment where each task receives the attention and dedication it deserves.

Team Exercise

Reflect with your team on its workload of the last two months, especially the number of simultaneously developed features, so-called work-in-progress, and the work finished. Discuss how work-in-progress impacts the completion of work items. Agree on work-in-progress limits and team activities to support each other in finishing a task before starting another. Do this exercise at least every month to understand new insights.

BEING DONE IS A MUTUAL AGREEMENT

You are done with your work only
if a commonly agreed definition says so.

Context

While working on work packages, it is essential that all team members, as well as stakeholders, have a unified definition of what 'done' means. Without this consensus, our teams risk facing misalignments that can lead to delays, compromised quality, or customer dissatisfaction.

We ensure that our teams have an upfront dialogue on the definition of done, internally and with their stakeholders. The clarity ensures that everyone involved has the same expectations and understands the criteria for completion. This minimises the potential for time-consuming debates and misunderstandings, ultimately leading to trust and higher productivity, as it streamlines the workflow and ensures that all efforts are directed towards meeting these established agreements.

Team Exercise

Discuss the current criteria to call a work package as done with your team. Then, break into small groups and let each group illustrate their understanding of the criteria through a painting. Set up a gallery walk and allow team members to comment on the artwork, placing sticky notes with thoughts and ideas. Synthesise together and agree on (improved) criteria.

WHAT GETS MEASURED, GETS MANAGED

Agile uses measurements to continuously improve.

Context

By quantitatively assessing various aspects of our teams' work, we gain objective insights and can make informed decisions based on actual data rather than assumptions. It is crucial not to just focus on one measurement but to consider a range of dimensions (e.g. quality, efficiency, value etc.), finding the right number of metrics to focus on the essentials of our success.

Encouraging teams to not only define metrics but also actively experiment with strategies to influence these figures is key. This approach enables continuous improvement, as teams can see the direct impact of their efforts on measurable outcomes. Reviewing and adjusting these measurements ensures they align with team goals and organisational objectives.

Team Exercise

Brainstorm and prioritise the team's success measurements (e.g. customer satisfaction, system uptime, etc.) and place them on a whiteboard. Discuss all measurements, considering data availability, maintenance, and effectiveness, and agree on a small set. Assign accountability and let the accountable team members present measurements regularly and discuss how to improve them.

DECISIONS MAKE
THE DRUMBEAT

Your organisation is as fast as its decision-making habits.

Context

A team can just move as fast as decisions are taken. In traditional settings, leaders often serve as the primary decision-makers, becoming bottlenecks and slowing down team progress. In an Agile environment, we, as leaders, want to drive decentralised decision-making. The decisions should be taken where the knowledge is, typically with the team.

As leaders, our role transforms into facilitating this empowerment, guiding our teams towards greater autonomy and self-organisation. This shift accelerates the decision-making process and consequently enhances the teams' throughput and efficiency. We enable a more dynamic and responsive work rhythm by removing ourselves as the bottleneck.

Team Exercise

List and analyse all your and your team's regularly made decisions, understanding the context for and the impact of the decisions. Cluster decisions into centralised and de-centralised and identify who has the accountability and suitable context to make decisions. Refine accountabilities together with the team and apply them going forward, regularly reflecting and improving if necessary.

KEEP YOUR EYES ON THE PRIZE

Work focused towards your objectives.

Context

In today's work environment, teams frequently face the challenge of being pulled in various directions, trying to satisfy multiple stakeholders. Having numerous tasks with different priorities being initiated simultaneously often results in a loss of focus, ultimately leading to decreased efficiency.

To mitigate this, we need to support our teams in not becoming overwhelmed by a multitude of requests and distractions. One effective strategy is establishing clear, short-term goals aligning with the team's overarching mission. By setting specific objectives, making the team accountable and channelling efforts towards achieving them, teams can remain concentrated on their central mission.

Team Exercise

Reflect with the team on the achieved iteration goals of the last two months. Compare the achievement of the iteration goal against the finalisation of the committed features and tasks and discuss how finishing all features and tasks might not necessarily contribute to the iteration goal and vice-versa. Identify improvements to balance finalising committed features and tasks and achieving the iteration goal.

FOCUS ON
IMPROVEMENT

Agile teams, navigating rapidly changing environments, anchor themselves in a culture committed to continuous improvement. This mindset is rooted in a deep dedication to personal and collective team growth. It involves a relentless pursuit of knowledge and skills, ensuring that individuals and the team evolve in tandem with their dynamic environment.

Fostering this culture needs more than just good intentions. It requires the right environment for growth. Teams need a safe space for learning, where experimentation is encouraged, and time is dedicated to development. This involves actively stretching beyond comfort zones and challenging the status quo. Key to this culture is regular feedback, continuous reflection and an emphasis on collaboration and shared learning. By sharing knowledge and experiences, team members contribute to a collective wisdom that ultimately propels the entire team forward.

Continuous improvement in Agile teams is about embracing learning as a never-ending journey. Failures and setbacks are reframed as valuable lessons, fuelling personal growth, resilience, and a relentless drive to excel and innovate. By embedding this culture of constant learning, feedback, and adaptability, teams do more than just respond to change. They anticipate and shape it, contributing to team success and advancement.

LEARN TO UNLEARN

Let go of certain habits, to be able to grow.

Context

Outdated behaviours and practices can hinder a team's ability to collaborate effectively and to align with evolving customer needs. Therefore, unlearning outdated behaviours is crucial for us and our teams.

We can support our teams in effectively unlearning by conducting regular team retrospectives to assess practices, mindsets, and behaviours and critically ask if they still support the team. This process creates room for adopting new, more effective behaviours and methodologies. Embracing new methods while celebrating and reinforcing positive changes motivates our teams to let go of the old. This continuous evolution and learning culture enables our teams to stay aligned with the latest industry trends and customer expectations, making them more effective and innovative.

Team Exercise

Conduct an unlearning exercise. Design a small labyrinth with a set of checkpoints on paper. Create cards with the team's outdated beliefs. Let team members navigate the maze. Whenever they get to a checkpoint, they should draw a card. The team must identify old habits for written belief and replace them with new, more suitable ones. Conclude the exercise with a reflection. Repeat this exercise regularly to foster unlearning behaviour.

GROWTH IS THE ANSWER TO CHANGE

Embracing a growth mindset helps you to conquer challenges ahead.

Context

A growth mindset is the belief that abilities can be developed through dedication and hard work. Such a mindset helps us and our teams to see obstacles as stepping stones for growth, mistakes as opportunities for learning, and uncertainties as a possibility to define the future.

As leaders, we are responsible for cultivating this mindset by encouraging a culture of curiosity and focusing on solution-oriented thinking rather than dwelling on problems. We need to provide ample learning resources and opportunities for professional development. Additionally, we can set stretch challenges that push team members beyond their comfort zones, fostering resilience and adaptability.

Team Exercise

Create and maintain a 'growth wall' where each team member is encouraged to contribute a weekly account of their personal growth experiences. Foster discussions on these entries during coffee breaks to promote a culture of continuous learning and development. Regularly inspect and adapt the 'growth wall' in reflection meetings and share your experience with other leaders and teams.

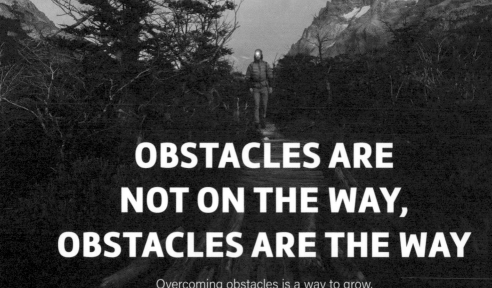

**OBSTACLES ARE
NOT ON THE WAY,
OBSTACLES ARE THE WAY**

Overcoming obstacles is a way to grow.

Context

Transforming established processes and charting uncharted territories is a challenging undertaking. On our journey of continuous improvement, we and our teams inevitably encounter impediments along the way, often more frequently than we would like. Rather than becoming discouraged, we should view these obstacles as stepping stones towards a better future.

We need to ensure that our teams recognise that obstacles are not detours but integral parts of the path, while working through each impediment often brings greater clarity and understanding of the overall journey.

Team Exercise

Reflect with your team on the most significant obstacles of the last two months. Discuss how you have overcome them and how this can help you with future and upcoming impediments. Agree on action items, either in the form of required behaviour among team members or a method which team members use for certain types of obstacles. In future, whenever the team overcomes an obstacle, celebrate it accordingly.

EVERY FAILURE
IS A LEARNING

Failing in a safe environment fosters growth.

Context

We should guide our teams to embrace the concept that every failure offers opportunities for growth and improvement. When mistakes occur, it is essential to approach them as learning experiences which bring clarity or prevent future missteps. By analysing the root causes of failures or extracting key lessons, we are better prepared for the future. Moreover, when these learnings are shared within the team and beyond, they become a resource for collective growth.

As leaders, we must not just promote such behaviours but also focus on creating a safe space where team members feel comfortable sharing learnings and taking risks, which permit or even encourage failure.

Team Exercise

Set up a monthly one-hour-long so-called f***-up meeting. Let your team members share mistakes, blunders, or failures they have experienced and the lessons they have learned from those incidents. Have them emphasise the learning process and what they changed to avoid those mistakes in the future. Facilitate the meeting, ensuring avoidance of shame or blame.

FEEDBACK
DRIVES PROGRESS

Every feedback loop makes your product better.

Context

Feedback is the compass that guides Agile teams toward continuous improvement. It is a critical link between the team and its users, revealing how the product is perceived and where enhancements are needed. This valuable input can come from diverse sources and data points, including user testing, customer reviews, or data analysis. With each piece of feedback, our teams can unlock opportunities for progress. They should engage in an iterative process, consistently refining their product to enhance customer satisfaction. Feedback becomes the catalyst for driving innovation, ensuring that our teams remain responsive to user needs and deliver ever-improving solutions.

Team Exercise

Assess together with your team your feedback collection process. Begin by evaluating how frequently you collect feedback, the sources you tap into, the stakeholders, and the channels through which feedback is acquired. Identify areas that need enhancement within these dimensions. Formulate actions to optimise your feedback gathering.

HONEST FEEDBACK FUELS TRUST

Agile teams embrace an open feedback culture.

Context

Honest feedback builds trust within an Agile team. It allows team members to be vulnerable and feel comfortable sharing their thoughts and ideas, creating a stronger team bond and a more collaborative and inclusive team culture. Honest feedback also shows team members that their colleagues and leaders are willing to be open and transparent with them, which can create a sense of mutual respect and understanding within the team. Trust is a crucial component of an effective Agile team, and honest feedback is integral to building and maintaining that trust.

Team Exercise

Organise a team feedback session in which each team member receives feedback from their peers. Before the session, provide specific guiding questions upfront (e.g. 'why is this team member important for us?', 'what advice do we offer them for future growth?', etc.) and ensure that all team members prepare their feedback.

BE GREATER TO DELIVER STRONGER

To deliver better and sooner, you should strive to perfect your ways of delivering.

Context

Continuous improvement of our delivery process is crucial for our teams to deliver highly qualitative work to our customers efficiently. This pursuit of excellence involves a relentless focus on refining processes, systems, methodologies, and tools. To drive this continuous improvement, teams should actively seek and utilise feedback.

We should encourage our teams to self-reflect and engage in a dialogue with customers and other organisation members to find improvement potential. Our teams should view every initiative and task as an opportunity to improve and grow, ensuring that the delivery process is not static but dynamically evolves to meet changing requirements and challenges.

Team Exercise

Conduct an improvement challenge with your team and stakeholders. Collect delivery process pain points, bottlenecks, and dependencies, if possible, underpinned by facts and data. Split participants into small groups and assign pain points, bottlenecks, and dependencies with the homework to discover innovative ways to resolve them. Collect, prioritise and implement all ideas and reward the group with the best idea.

STEAL AND TWEAK

Rather than continually striving to create fresh concepts,
consider refining or blending existing ones.

Context

Our ever-faster world requires us to realise value fast. Reusing existing ideas offers swift value delivery in a resource-efficient way. It makes organisations more successful and helps in preserving institutional knowledge. To do so, we and our teams must maintain a repository of past initiatives and encourage knowledge sharing. We should encourage team members to build upon the foundations laid by their colleagues.

Additionally, it is crucial to promote an outward-looking approach. Often, solutions to team-internal challenges can be found externally, sometimes even outside of the organisation. We need to embrace ideas, approaches and concepts from other sources and tweak them to our environment.

Team Exercise

Create and maintain a repository of design ideas and solutions to challenges from past projects. Conduct a recurring idea-reuse meeting with your team in the following manner. Form groups of three and let them discuss and merge ideas and solutions from the repository into new concepts. Let the groups present in a debrief and plan how to use the new concepts.

DELIVER WITH HEART, ANALYSE WITH MIND

Trust your instincts when you design and deliver, trust your numbers when you inspect and adapt.

Context

Agile teams aim to deliver value in a fast and incremental way. To do so, we ensure that our teams do not overthink, are creative and trust their instincts. For that, it is critical to timebox discussions, make incremental decisions, embrace imperfection, and seek real-world feedback.

On the other hand, collecting and analysing data enables us to drive continuous improvement, make informed decisions, and align with business goals. Feedback mechanisms and regular review meetings ensure valuable insights are gathered and integrated systematically, optimising output. A good balance between these two stances drives our teams' success.

Team Exercise

Conduct an analysis instinct balance workshop, letting team members reflect on the last two months by sticking their notes to either the INSTINCT or ANALYSIS column and noting triggers next to the notes. Let the team analyse the notes and triggers and define strategies to maintain a healthy balance between the two stances.

EXPERIMENTS
NEVER FAIL

Experimentation is the best way to uncover the truth.

Context

Experiments play a crucial role in fostering a culture of continuous improvement. They allow our teams to explore and test new ideas in a practical setting. When the outcome of an experiment is positive, it can lead to enhancements in products or a better way of working. Equally important, a negative outcome provides insights into what does not work, guiding teams towards alternative solutions. Therefore, every experiment, irrespective of its result, is valuable.

Embracing this experimental mindset allows teams to innovate and try new approaches without the fear of failure, knowing that each attempt, successful or not, contributes to their growth and understanding.

Team Exercise

Set up an experimentation challenge, where you challenge your team to run at least one experiment per week. Record the number of experiments and outcomes. Celebrate positive and negative results to foster a culture of learning. Extend this challenge to your leadership peers, encouraging them to implement similar practices with their teams. Set up an EXPERIMENT BOARD to display the progress of all teams.

WORK ON THE SYSTEM
SO YOU CAN BETTER
WORK IN THE SYSTEM

To become more efficient and effective,
continuously improve your system.

Context

Teams are often consumed with delivering work and do not have time to reflect on how they deliver work. As leaders, we help our teams to become more effective and efficient by applying a feedback loop approach not only to enhance the product but also to refine the system within which they operate, including processes, tools, collaboration and communication methods, as well as established habits. We do so by ensuring reflection and giving our teams the necessary time and space for it. Through iterative reflection and incremental improvement within short feedback loops, our teams optimise the overall system.

Team Exercise

Establish a regular retrospective meeting where the team discusses how the system can be improved. Follow the pattern, 'what to start?' 'what to stop?' and 'what to continue?' Cluster improvements into team and system buckets. Focus on selecting team improvements and prioritising quality over quantity. Address system improvements with other team leaders and discuss prioritisation and implementation.

ACKNOWLEDGEMENTS

Our journey into the Agile world began over a decade ago, a journey that has profoundly influenced the creation of this book. Along the way, we have been fortunate to encounter many inspiring mentors, great leaders, challenging clients, and supportive colleagues. Each has played a crucial role in elevating our thinking, shaping our perspectives, and broadening our horizons. We are immensely thankful for their insights and impulses. Without their influence, this book would not have materialized.

About one and a half years ago, the idea for this book emerged, initially as a random thought, often mentioned in jest. However, with the encouragement of many friends and colleagues, what started as a joke became a serious endeavour. As a core team, we came together to distil a decade's worth of knowledge and experiences into these pages.

Our creative journey has been interspersed with life's remarkable events, the joy of welcoming a new child into the world, the celebration of a beautiful marriage, and a globe-spanning relocation from Zurich to Brazil and via Bali back to Zurich. Despite these significant personal events, we always kept the focus. Through countless calls across continents, many late evening sessions after intense workdays, a team expansion and weekend sessions, we adhered to our ambitious timeline. All this was achievable only through the unwavering support of our families and friends, who sacrificed their time with us to complete this book.

In closing, we would like to extend our heartfelt gratitude to everyone who stood by us. This book is a testament to your support, and it is to you we would like to express our deepest thank you:

- Natascha and Ilona, for your belief in us, for being the catalyst in starting this writing journey and for always being there for us.

- Núria, for always bringing a smile on our face.

- Ivy, for your boundless energy, playful spirit and loving nature.

- Jan and Jan, for serving as a continuous source of inspiration and for fostering a healthy sibling rivalry that has been a natural motivator.

- Our families, for your steadfast presence and support.

- Marcel and Alex, for a decade of guidance, counselling, and mentorship.

- Stephanie and Kirsten for such inspiring leadership.

- Jannick, for providing insightful feedback on our early drafts.

- All our friends and colleagues who, knowingly or unknowingly, contributed to quotes and exercises with their knowledge and wisdom.

- The ones in front of the camera, living their essence as a source of inspiration to the world around them.

- All those who invested time to review, give feedback and share their external perspectives on the whole.

- Harm and Peter, for your faith in us and for the invaluable support and guidance in publishing our first book.

Your collective support and inspiration have been the very backbone of this journey. For that, we are profoundly and sincerely grateful.

CREATORS

Jérôme, the Enthusiast

Over the last ten years, I have dedicated myself to guiding individuals, teams, and organizations along their Agile transformation journey. In my role as an advisor and coach to many, my constant goal has been to inspire everyone I work with to adopt a true Agile culture.

Anton, the Sophist

I love all kinds of thought experiments and the sharing of those. Once I have thought something through, it is essential for me to articulate myself in the most understandable and comprehensive way, whether in the form of a metaphor, comparison, or structured definition.

Maja, the Artist
I have been dedicating the past years to telling stories and creating impact through images. As a psychology and philosophy lover, combined with my business background and self-taught photography skills, I strive to use art as a way to express ideas.

Ladislav, the Designer
Bringing ideas to life in the most creative and efficient way is what excites me. I enjoy the process of creation, be it a beautiful painting, useful software, or an insightful book. In a complex world like ours, it is important to be clear about for whom and for what we create.

To learn more visit our website:
https://www.wisdomofagile.com